Notes on Our Times

E. B. WHITE

Notes on Our Times

Foreword by Paul Saffo

Illustrations by Edward Barbini

LEVENGER PRESS

Published by
Levenger Press
420 South Congress Avenue
Delray Beach, Florida 33445 USA
Levengerpress.com 800.544.0880

Published by permission of Allene White, the successor in interest to E. B. White, by whom copyright in the work published herein is retained and all rights are reserved. No part of the work of E. B. White in this book may be reproduced in any form or by any means without permission in writing.

Foreword © 2007 by Paul Saffo. All rights reserved.

Library of Congress Cataloging-in-Publication Data

White, E. B. (Elwyn Brooks), 1899-1985.
  Notes on our times / E. B. White ; foreword by Paul Saffo ; illustrations by Edward Barbini.
     p. cm.
  A collection of essays.
  Includes bibliographical references.
  ISBN-13: 978-1-929154-30-2
  I. Barbini, Edward. II. Title.
  PS3545.H5187N67 2007
  814'.52--dc22

2007026283

Cover and book design by Danielle Furci
Mim Harrison, Editor

Contents

Foreword	IX

Notes on Our Times

Mrs. Wienckus	1
Rainmakers	5
The Dream of the American Male	11
Biographee	17
Country Dwellers	21
Professor Piccard	25
The Home	31
Censorship	35
Sound	39
The Age of Dust	45
Trance	51
Cowboy	55
Heavier Than Air	59
Railroads	67
Mantis	71
Withholding	75
Nails	79
Crab Grass	83
Remembrance of Things Past	87
Experimentation	91
Daylight and Darkness	95
Air Raid Drill	99
The Distant Music of the Hounds	107
The Photographs	114

Foreword

Future Past and Future Present

> This focus on the universal human experience does not merely make White relevant today—it is what gives these essays their predictive power.

Foreword

Oracles move among us unnoticed, their plainspoken auguries hidden in the murmur of daily life, overlooked by all but the most astute of listeners. Over his many decades with *The New Yorker*, E. B. White became just such a listener as he wrote his incisive essays for the magazine's Notes and Comment page.

The essays in this collection first appeared in *The New Yorker* between 1937 and 1952, an interval framed by a waning Great Depression on one end and a waxing Cold War on the other. In between were the Holocaust, World War II, the atomic bomb, Walt Disney, the Iron Curtain, Chuck Yeager, television, the United Nations, and, barely noticed, the invention of the transistor and birth of the modern electronic age. Even when compared with events today, it was a period of unprecedented tumult and uncertainty.

It was also a period when writers were not afraid to tackle the big issues head-on in print, as experts filled editorial pages and bookstores with their prescriptions for meeting the great

Foreword

challenges of the time. In contrast to these top-down explicators, White worked up from the specific in his understated way, leading the reader to a conclusion so self-evident by essay's end that he barely needed to mention it. "The Age of Dust" is an especially elegant example, gently revealing the lunatic, Strangelovian illogic of radiological warfare with references to a swing, a little girl and her handkerchief.

White writes about what the poet Robinson Jeffers called "permanent things." The garden-mad "department-store peasantry" depicted in "Country Dwellers" are still among us, driving SUVs instead of station wagons and relying on the Web and FedEx to deliver their wooden armchairs and pearwood soap dishes. This focus on the universal human experience does not merely make White relevant today—it is what gives these essays their predictive power, for the novelties that so surprise us are inevitably the expression of unchanging human hopes and fears, follies and desires.

Foreword

White writes about perennial human truths, but one must read these essays more than once to fully appreciate their timelessness. On first reading, give in to the inevitable desire to focus on mention of the unfamiliar: a Victrola, a Pullman berth, or a now-ancient Convair turboprop airliner. The first time through, the description of a modern pig nursery in "Remembrance of Things Past" is arresting for its mention of a long-obsolete piglet-comforting Victrola. But read again, the piece presages the issues surrounding humankind's separation from nature and the safety of livestock antibiotics, issues that remain pressing concerns today.

Mark Twain is said to have observed that history doesn't repeat itself, but sometimes it rhymes. One such parallel can be found in White's description of stratospheric explorer Jean Piccard's 1937 trip into the blue, hanging from 92 latex balloons: it anticipates the 1982 flight of one Larry Walters from Long Beach, California, who floated over Los Angeles at 16,000 feet in a lawn chair suspended from forty-two weather balloons. Like

Foreword

Piccard, Walters initiated his descent by carefully shooting out one balloon after another, as the pilots of passing airliners on approach to LAX looked on in astonishment. The constant, of course, is the intrinsic nuttiness of humans, be they madcap professors (Piccard's twin brother was, in fact, the inspiration for Professor Calculus in Hervé's *Tintin* books) or California free spirits hoping to cross the continent on the jet stream. As White observes in the final essay of this collection, "Man's inventions, directed always onward and upward, have an odd way of leading back to man himself...."

White's oracular side pops up repeatedly in these essays. I recalled his "Age of Dust" meditation with a shudder when I first learned of Alexander Litvinenko's 2006 poisoning by polonium. And in "Censorship," Janet Jackson's 2004 "wardrobe malfunction" is foreshadowed in White's commentary on a 1939 ruling that one female breast, but not two, could be exposed at the 1939 World's Fair "World of Tomorrow." Americans' fretting over things moral is, it seems,

Foreword

a constant. These examples may be lucky hits, but in other instances, White's prescience feels more than coincidental. In "Rainmakers," he observes, "New York's water shortage is caused less by lack of rain than by lack of foresight, lack of a decent feeling for nature." If only our public servants had taken White's comment to heart when he wrote these prophetic words, perhaps we would now be better prepared for the gathering crisis of global climate change.

The Greeks revered their oracles because their utterances inevitably invited petitioners to look inside themselves for an answer. This is where White is at his very best, framing his essays in a way that all but compels introspection. "Sound" explores the impact of radio and long-forgotten political sound trucks, but it also speaks eloquently to the challenges raised by today's tumultuous digital media revolution. White's observation that "amplification, therefore, is something like alcohol: it can heighten our meanings, but it can also destroy our reason" resonates with worries today regarding the impact

Foreword

of the vast chatter in the blogosphere or the studied vulgarity of talk show hosts competing for listener attention.

Each of the essays printed here offers similar invitations to shine a distant mirror on the future. The predicament of Mrs. Wienckus, a well-off, hard-working domestic who is arrested for sleeping in a hallway, parallels that of today's working poor who live in gypsy RVs surreptitiously parked on the streets of wealthy California beach suburbs. White's musing on the impromptu water landing of an off-course Northeast Airlines Convair, and the subsequent chiding from a "time-fitted" TWA pilot comfortably peering into a future that's arriving at two miles a minute, both anticipate today's debates over the reliability of the ever-more advanced technologies that hold our lives in the balance. In the same essay, "Heavier Than Air," White refers to the "new normalcy," an eerie anticipation of the "new normal," a neologism popular immediately after the dot-com crash earlier in this decade.

Foreword

These essays are a compelling reminder that no matter how formal the method, or formidable the analytic tool, all forecasts worth their salt are underpinned by careful observation of the overlooked present and a willingness to swim against the stream of popular consciousness and opinion. In this age when the Web and myriad new media make it harder than ever to drown out the din of the present, I keep E. B. White close by as a reminder of what is truly important: the long view.

In the course of exploring White's expository revelations, I carried these essays on more trips than I recall, covering more miles than I remember. His observations have resonated in surprising ways with the geographies I traversed. I reread "The Dream of the American Male" after a visit to one of our larger army bases, and although the essay's description of a soldier's feminine ideal might raise eyebrows today, its sentiment rings true in the milieu of young warriors riding into battle in Humvees and Blackhawks.

Foreword

I suggest you carry this book with you, allowing the connection between what is on its pages and what you see in the world to heighten your sense of the future as well as your appreciation of the past. In another book by E. B. White, Stuart Little asks his classmates, "How many of you know what's important?" These essays are not only White's eloquent answer to that question, but also an invitation to ask that question of ourselves.

Paul Saffo
Silicon Valley
September 2007

Mrs. Wienckus

> Mrs. Wienckus interests us because her "disorderliness" was simply her capacity to live a far more self-contained life than most of us can manage.

Notes on Our Times

The Newark police arrested a very interesting woman the other day—a Mrs. Sophie Wienckus—and she is now on probation after being arraigned as disorderly. Mrs. Wienckus interests us because her "disorderliness" was simply her capacity to live a far more self-contained life than most of us can manage. The police complained that she was asleep in two empty cartons in a hallway. This was her preferred method of bedding down. All the clothes she possessed she had on—several layers of coats and sweaters. On her person were bankbooks showing that she was ahead of the game to the amount of $19,799.09. She was a working woman—a domestic—and, on the evidence, a thrifty one. Her fault, the Court held, was that she lacked a habitation.

"Why didn't you rent a room?" asked the magistrate. But he should have added parenthetically "(and the coat hangers in the closet and the cord that pulls the light and the dish that holds the soap and the mirror that conceals the cabinet where lives the aspirin that kills the pain)." Why didn't you rent a room "(with the rug that collects the dirt and the vacuum that sucks the dirt

3

E.B. WHITE

and the man that fixes the vacuum and the fringe that adorns the shade that dims the lamp and the desk that holds the bill for the installment on the television set that tells of the wars)?" We feel that the magistrate oversimplified his question.

Mrs. Wienckus may be disorderly, but one pauses to wonder where the essential disorder really lies. All of us are instructed to seek hallways these days (except school children, who crawl under the desks), and it was in a hallway that they found Mrs. Wienckus, all compact. We read recently that the only hope of avoiding inflation is through ever increasing production of goods. This to us is always a terrifying conception of the social order—a theory of the good life through accumulation of objects. We lean toward the order of Mrs. Wienckus, who has eliminated everything except what she can conveniently carry, whose financial position is solid, and who can smile at Rufus Rastus Johnson Brown. We salute a woman whose affairs are in such excellent order in a world untidy beyond all belief.

Rainmakers

It is entirely in keeping with man's feeling about nature that when he suddenly notices his drinking fountain losing pressure, he should ascend to heaven and beat a cloud over the ears.

Notes on Our Times

When he was told that people were bringing suit against the makers of rain, Mayor O'Dwyer, the rainmaker, said, "Somebody doesn't want it to rain, I take it." This remark belongs right up with the more cocky utterances of self-reliant man, alongside Hague's famous pronouncement: "I am the law." It was almost as though the Mayor had said, "I am the rain." By putting in their place those who took an opposite view of rain, he reduced precipitation to simple dogma. His was not a demagogic remark, like Hague's—simply an Olympian remark, innocent and infinitely remote. Somebody indeed doesn't want it to rain—some almost, but not quite, forgotten man. How about this fellow? He interests us. Crotchety, probably. Or maybe an inveterate picnicker. But a man, nevertheless—two arms, two legs, an umbrella, and a habit of looking to the limitless sky for his rewards and punishments, not to a city father.

An arresting quality in modern man is his attitude toward his natural surroundings, a quality likely to get him in trouble

E. B. WHITE

and even shorten his stay on earth. He commonly thinks of himself as having been here since the beginning—older than the crab—and he also likes to think he's destined to stay to the bitter end. Actually, he is a late comer, and there are moments when he shows every sign of being an early leaver—a patron who bows out after a few gaudy and memorable scenes. It is entirely in keeping with man's feeling about nature that when he suddenly notices his drinking fountain losing pressure, he should ascend to heaven and beat a cloud over the ears. Petulance, coupled with insatiable curiosity, and the will to dominate. "Somebody doesn't want it to rain, I take it," said the Mayor, while the lightning played all around his words.

The city presumably feels it has a pretty good legal loophole. Even if a plane goes up and seeds a cloud, and rain falls, the wet people down below will have to prove that the seed germinated, that the rain was in fact the fruit of the seed. This may be hard to prove. Legally, rainmaking may be in the clear as a device. Philosophically, rainmaking is anything but in the

Notes on Our Times

clear—it is in a misty mid-region. There is more to rain than meets the kitchen tap of a city dweller; rain is part of the stuff of melancholia, part of darkness, of husbandry, of sport, and of retailing. Everyone talks about the weather because the weather is every man's chattel. The suicide often holds off until it rains, and the pilot who seeds a cloud may be seeding a man, too, and causing the ultimate and unbearable teardrop. The rain pilot's flight is a long, long flight—into the wild gray yonder.

New York's water shortage is caused less by lack of rain than by lack of foresight, lack of a decent feeling for nature. The remedy, it seems to us, is not the manufacture of rain but the correct use and distribution of whatever rain naturally arrives on earth. If, as the rainmakers would have it, man does invade the sky and nudge clouds, his flight will, we predict, be but the beginning of such practices, and we shall find the makers of lightning also aloft, to satisfy the desires of the manufacturers of lightning rods, who may decide that lightning is in short supply and devise a way of setting more of it loose. This, in turn, will be an affront to insurance companies, who must stand the cost of retopping chimneys that get hit by the bolts. In short, it is conceivable that man may have to set an arbitrary limit to his domain—draw a line where he ends and God begins. The Mayor may think he is the rain, but when he pours he may have a surprise coming.

The Dream of
the American Male

> If you know what a soldier wants, you know what Man wants, for a soldier is caught in a line of work which leads toward a distant and tragic conclusion.

Notes on Our Times

Dorothy Lamour is the girl above all others desired by the men in Army camps. This fact was turned up by *Life* in a routine study of the unlimited national emergency. It is a fact which illuminates the war, the national dream, and our common unfulfillment. If you know what a soldier wants, you know what Man wants, for a soldier is young, sexually vigorous, and is caught in a line of work which leads toward a distant and tragic conclusion. He personifies Man. His dream of a woman can be said to be Everyman's dream of a woman. In desiring Lamour, obviously his longing is for a female creature encountered under primitive conditions and in a setting of great natural beauty and mystery. He does not want this woman to make any sudden or nervous movement. She should be in a glade, a swale, a grove, or a pool below a waterfall. This is the setting in which every American youth first encountered Miss Lamour. They were in a forest; she had walked slowly out of the pool and stood dripping in the ferns.

E.B. WHITE

The dream of the American male is for a female who has an essential languor which is not laziness, who is unaccompanied except by himself, and who does not let him down. He desires a beautiful, but comprehensible, creature who does not destroy a perfect situation by forming a complete sentence. She is compounded of moonlight and shadows, and has a slightly husky voice, which she uses only in song or in an attempt to pick up a word or two that he teaches her. Her body, if concealed at all, is concealed by a water lily, a frond, a fern, a bit of moss, or by a sarong—which is a simple garment carrying the implicit promise that it will not long stay in place. For millions of years men everywhere have longed for Dorothy Lamour. Now, in the final complexity of an age which has reached its highest expression in the instrument panel of a long-range bomber, it is a good idea to remember that Man's most persistent dream is of a forest pool and a girl coming out of it unashamed, walking toward him with a wavy motion, childlike in her wonder, a girl exquisitely untroubled, as quiet

Notes on Our Times

and accommodating and beautiful as a young green tree. That's all he really wants. He sometimes wonders how this other stuff got in—the instrument panel, the night sky, the full load, the moment of exultation over the blackened city below....

Biographee

> A great many of the most consistently indolent characters in the United States are listed in *Who's Who*, and some of them haven't felt an ounce of pressure since 1910.

Notes on Our Times

We have a letter this morning from Wheeler Sammons, publisher of *Who's Who in America*. It is a long, chatty letter, full of shoptalk. He speaks intimately of his "next scheduled stuffing," of the "currency-of-content provided by the biographee's coöperation," and of "revisionary data." The thing that impresses us particularly about this letter from Mr. Sammons (and we have had many others) is his introductory remark. He starts with an apology: "…I appreciate your every moment is under pressure."

Mr. Sammons undoubtedly believes this to be true of his biographees, that their every moment is under pressure. He must think of himself as running a stable of thoroughbreds, in which there is no horse of no account, no horse that isn't terribly busy. But it is a delusion, a dream. A great many of the most consistently indolent characters in the United States are listed in *Who's Who*, and some of them haven't felt an ounce of pressure since 1910, when their first book came out. They are men who have made their mark, have joined a club, and are

E.B. WHITE

content to let bygones be bygones. We speak with knowledge about this matter. A biographee of no small inactivity ourself, we can state positively that we are under no pressure at the moment—except the tiny pressure connected with writing this ephemeral paragraph. After it is done, we intend to walk slowly to Central Park in the mild sunshine and visit the baby camel for a routine checkup, then to a saloon, where we shall pass the early afternoon hours in deep torpor over a glass of May wine—a biographee as near inert as a horned toad.

Country Dwellers

> Of country living, which they know only hurriedly, they make a sort of masque, dressing for a walk-on part in the play Nature.

Notes on Our Times

People are retreating to the deep country in these June days, fleeing the heat, searching for roots, a department-store peasantry in slacks and espadrilles, ploughing the fields of summer with their roan station wagons. Of country living, which they know only hurriedly, they make a sort of masque, dressing for a walk-on part in the play Nature. "Dig in the garden," says *Vogue*, "in a Chinese laundryman's jumper of blue or white cotton, pulled over trousers to match or over a cotton skirt. Keep all the scarfs you find in Mexico, Brittany, or Mittel-Europa. Order from Haiti the wooden armchairs with seats and backs of natural matting. And for your country bathroom, have rows of bottles covered in wicker cases and soap-dishes of bleached pearwood from Jean-Michel Frank." There is something almost frenzied in this advice to persons returning to the land—a frenzy which only half cloaks the strange guilt of the dispossessed. A dogwood tree is dragged down a hill behind a caterpillar tractor. A setting of duck eggs is rushed five hundred miles by motorcar to be placed under a hen. Nervous country dwellers, wistfully hoping to keep the world alive by rearranging its bloom and warming its embryos.

Professor Piccard— Before

The professor this time
will invade not only the
stratosphere but that
equally vaporous region,
the Realm of Probability.

Notes on Our Times

Professor Piccard, traveller in the outer spheres, has announced his intention of making another ascent, this time borne aloft by 2,000 small balloons instead of by one big one. If he carries out his plan, the trip should be of profound interest to logicians—for the professor this time will invade not only the stratosphere but that equally vaporous region, the Realm of Probability. Usually, you see, the Professor relies, for his descent, on letting some gas out of his bag; but on this occasion he will rely on the fitful bursting of some of the little balloons in the rarefied air to which they are exposed. He hopes that only "some" of the little balloons, not all of them, will give way, and feels that probability is on his side.

The calculation of probability has long occupied the night thoughts of gambling men, and the coin-flippers of the world will brood endlessly on the idea of 2,000 little supporting balloons, some of which must hold, some of which must let go. What, they will want to know, are the chances of having 2,000 balloons, all subjected to bursting conditions, explode at comfortable intervals? It is not probable, yet it is conceivable, that 2,000 balloons, rising into an unfavorable zone, might explode as one, just as it is conceivable that a coin, tossed fifty times, might show heads in all fifty flips. And there is still another, larger question which comes up, it seems to us: What effect does rarefied air have on the very law itself? Can anyone state, authoritatively, that there exists any such thing as probability so far from the core of earth? We wish Dr. Abraham Wolf and Dr. William Fleetwood Sheppard, who wrote the fascinating chapters on probability in the Britannica, would write us an equation covering the probable interval of explosion of 2,000 little balloons dangling an inquisitive professor in the already improbable blue.

Professor Piccard—After

Dr. Piccard, of the upper air, brings to scientific fields the highest quality of madness. This sprightly little explorer, the jackanapes of the stratosphere, cunningly soars aloft in a basket

Notes on Our Times

borne upward by a galaxy of toy balloons, suddenly whips out a gun and takes pot shots at his own supports. "So I took my pistol and killed about a dozen of them," he explained. It was the sort of plot Harpo Marx might hatch, with his hair straying and his eyes too bright. Dr. Piccard descended in flames, and when he jumped out, according to the papers, he was choked with laughter.

The Home

Home was quite a place

when people stayed there.

Notes on Our Times

Homemaking reared its chintzy little head the other day when the ladies of the American Home Economics Association decided that maybe the Home should rate a Cabinet position, to be called the Department of the American Home. It is a noble idea and would unquestionably attract the wrong people. If we had a Secretary of the Home, like a Secretary of State or a Secretary of Commerce, she would probably be a lady whose emphasis would be upon vitamins and lampshades. She would be against mice. The American Home, given Cabinet status, would continue to move (as it has moved in the last few years) in the wrong direction. The American Kitchen would become more and more stagy and unlivable; the American Cellar would finally and forever emerge as a rumpus room, above ground; the Home as a whole would tend to become collapsible, transparent, mobile, washable, sterile, and devoid of human life.

Home is too delicate an organism to be federalized. The eviction of even so small a thing as a mouse threatens its balance; the absence of a hummingbird from the delphiniums can destroy its tone. Some of the most vital and dependable homes we have ever been in were ones in which the economics were deplorable; some of the barest of homes were ones which, physically, were the answer to an economist's dream. Home was quite a place when people stayed there, but Home Economics is just another in the long line of activities that take ladies away. Of the home economists we have met in our lifetime, all had one trait in common: not one of them was at home.

Censorship

> This harem-but-no-sultan decision belongs in the truly great body of opinion interpreting the American moral law.

NOTES ON OUR TIMES

We are delighted with the recent censorship ruling in the matter of motion-picture harems. Some scenes in a Paramount picture now in production are set in a harem, and after careful deliberation the censors have decided to allow this type of polyform allure *provided* the boudoir does not contain the sultan. The girls can mill about among the pillows, back and side having gone bare, but no male eye must gaze upon them—save, of course, yours, lucky reader. This harem-but-no-sultan decision belongs in the truly great body of opinion interpreting the American moral law. It takes its place alongside the celebrated 1939 ruling on the exposure of female breasts in the Flushing World of Tomorrow, which provided that one breast could be presented publicly but not two, and thereby satisfied the two seemingly irreconcilable groups: the art-lovers, who demanded breasts but were willing to admit that if you'd seen one you'd seen them both, and the decency clique, who held out for concealment but were agreed that the fact of concealing one breast established the essential reticence of the owner and thereby covered the whole situation, or chest. That subtle and far-reaching ruling carried the Fair, as we know, safely through two difficult seasons, and we imagine that the aseptic harem will do as much for Hollywood.

Sound

> The rule seems to be:
> make sense if you can, but
> if you can't make sense
> say something anyway.

Notes on Our Times

The sound truck, or Free Speech on Wheels, won its first brush with the law by a close decision in the Supreme Court. We have an idea, however, that the theme of amplification is not dead and will recur in many variations. The Court found itself in a snarl; free speech became confused with free extension-of-speech, noise with ideas wrapped in noise. A sound truck, it seems to us, is not a man on a soapbox—it is Superman on a tower of suds. The distinction will eventually have to be drawn. Loud speaking is not the same thing as plain speaking; the loudspeaker piles decibel on decibel and not only is capable of disturbing the peace but through excess of volume can cause madness and death, whereas the human voice is a public nuisance only to the extent that it aggravates the normal human resentment against the whole principle of free speech. Amplified sound is already known among military men as a weapon of untried potency, and we will probably suffer from it if there is another war.

E.B. WHITE

Up till now, modern man has meekly accepted the miracle of his enlarged vocal cords. He has acquiesced in jumboism. A modern baby is born amplified, for even the nursery is wired for sound and the infant's earliest cries are carried over a private distress system to the ears of its mother in the living room—along with street noises that drift in through the open nursery window. (Note to political candidates: Always park your sound truck under nursery windows and your remarks will be picked up by an interior network and carried to uneasy elders.) One wonders, though, how much longer the human race will string along with its own electrical gifts, and how long the right to speak can remain innocent of wattage. We have a feeling that only if this issue is met will the principle of free speech survive. There are always plenty of people who are eager to stifle opinion they don't admire, and if the opinion happens to be expressed in a volume of sound that is in itself insufferable, the number of people who will want to stifle both the sound *and* the fury will greatly increase. Amplification,

Notes on Our Times

therefore, is something like alcohol: it can heighten our meanings, but it can also destroy our reason.

In radio it is understood that whatever else happens, there must never be a silence. This hard condition is most noticeable in the aerial forums, in which the performers are expected to offer an immediate opinion on any subject, and do. Someone must always be speaking, either the ringmaster or one of the experts. The rule seems to be: make sense if you can, but if you can't make sense say something anyway. If you listen to one of these nervous exercises in intellectual rough-and-tumble, it is plain that a large part of the effort goes simply into preventing a lull in the conversation. The Quakers take a more sensible view of silence; they accord it equal recognition with sound. We doubt that radio will ever amount to a damn as long as it is haunted by the fear of nobody speaking.

The Age of Dust

The terror of the atom age
is not the violence of the
new power but the speed
of man's adjustment to it.
Already bombproofing is
on approximately the same
level as mothproofing.

NOTES ON OUR TIMES

On a sunny morning last week, we went out and put up a swing for a little girl, age three, under an apple tree—the tree being much older than the girl, the sky being blue, the clouds white. We pushed the little girl for a few minutes, then returned to the house and settled down to an article on death dust, or radiological warfare, in the July *Bulletin of the Atomic Scientists*, Volume VI, No. 7.

The article ended on a note of disappointment. "The area that can be poisoned with the fission products available to us today is disappointingly small; it amounts to not more than two or three major cities per month." At first glance, the sentence sounded satirical, but a rereading convinced us that the scientist's disappointment was real enough—that it had the purity of detachment. The world of the child in the swing (the trip to the blue sky and back again) seemed, as we studied the ABC of death dust, more and more a dream world with no true relation to things as they are or to the real world of discouragement over the slow rate of the disappearance of cities.

E.B. WHITE

Probably the scientist-author of the death-dust article, if he were revising his literary labors with a critical eye, would change the wording of that queer sentence. But the fact is, the sentence got written and published. The terror of the atom age is not the violence of the new power but the speed of man's adjustment to it—the speed of his acceptance. Already bombproofing is on approximately the same level as mothproofing. Two or three major cities per month isn't much of an area, but it is a start. To the purity of science (which hopes to enlarge the area) there seems to be no corresponding purity of political thought, never the same detachment. We sorely need, from a delegate in the Security Council, a statement as detached in its way as the statement of the scientist on death dust. This delegate (and it makes no difference what nation he draws his pay from) must be a man who has not adjusted to the age of dust. He must be a person who still dwells in the mysterious dream world of swings, and little girls in

Notes on Our Times

swings. He must he more than a good chess player studying the future; he must be a memoirist remembering the past.

We couldn't seem to separate the little girl from radiological warfare—she seemed to belong with it, although inhabiting another sphere. The article kept getting back to her. "This is a novel type of warfare, in that it produces no destruction, except to life." The weapon, said the author, can be regarded as a horrid one, or, on the other hand, it "can be regarded as a remarkably humane one. In a sense, it gives each member of the target population [including each little girl] a choice of whether he will live or die." It turns out that the way to live—if that be your choice—is to leave the city as soon as the dust arrives, holding "a folded, dampened handkerchief" over your nose and mouth. We went outdoors again to push the swing some more for the little girl, who is always forgetting her handkerchief. At lunch we watched her try to fold her napkin. It seemed to take forever.

E.B. WHITE

As we lay in bed that night, thinking of cities and target populations, we saw the child again. This time she was with the other little girls in the subway. When the train got to 242nd Street, which is as far as it goes into unreality, the children got off. They started to walk slowly north. Each child had a handkerchief, and every handkerchief was properly moistened and folded neatly—the way it said in the story.

Trance

It is here, among the strange accoutrements of the horticultural life, that we forget, losing ourself completely. The senses float in pale regions of total intellectual stupor.

NOTES ON OUR TIMES

That delicious Sabbath trance induced by the study of the Sunday *Times* reaches its glassiest phase when we get into the changeless ads on the garden page of the Drama-Screen-Radio-Music-Dance-Art-Stamps-Resorts-Travel-Gardens-Women's News-Bridge Section. It is here, among the strange accoutrements of the horticultural life, that we forget, losing ourself completely. The senses float in pale regions of total intellectual stupor. A flexible blade to increase the efficiency of the lawn mower which we know we will never push over lawns measureless to man; a citronella candle to banish the imaginary mosquito from the imaginary porch on the fancied terrible summer night; twenty pachysandras for one dollar—how calm we feel, reading about them, how sweetly safe and indolent behind the walls of this stifling room in town! Here is a device for dehydrating vegetables, here a treatise on the breeding of earthworms for the feeding of hens in confinement, here a lovely silver gazing ball for the informal coppice. As our lids slowly droop, the scene expands and lightens, and we stand in the centre of this unearthly pleasure spot, this garden close, this green maze, with the cutworms and the laying pullets creeping around our feet, the liquid repellent for dogs and beetles gurgling over the mossy stones of the artificial brook, and an incredibly beautiful woman staring steadily into the gazing ball. No matter that this is the century of trouble: it is Sunday in the living room and there is a panacea for every ill.

Cowboy

> In this pendulous cowboy our
> century comes to a sort of head:
> the winged ranch hand, his eye
> on two steers at once, and the
> steers a thousand miles apart.

Notes on Our Times

We commend to historians the steer wrestler who has been commuting between Chicago and New York by plane, in order to throw steers in the rodeos of both cities. In this pendulous cowboy, if cowboy is the word for him, our century comes to a sort of head: the winged ranch hand, his eye on two steers at once, and the steers a thousand miles apart yet capable of being thrown by the winged, neither steer needing to be thrown, each existing only to be thrown. The cowboy rises from the head of the fallen animal, dusts the seat of his pants, walks stiff-legged to the waiting airliner. The spectators, yearning for the open West and its herds of cattle on the ranges, rise from their mezzanine seats, stiff-legged, dust off their unfulfilled desires, walk to the exits.

Heavier Than Air

The mental poise of this
airline pilot in the middle
of difficult flight shows
man's spirit maintaining
a small but significant lead
over his instrument panel.

Notes on Our Times

The first time we ever saw a large, heavy airplane drop swiftly out of the sky for a landing, we thought the maneuver had an element of madness in it. We haven't changed our opinion much in thirty years. During that time, to be sure, a great many planes have dropped down and landed successfully, and the feat is now generally considered to be practicable, even natural. Anyone who, like us, professes to find something implausible in it is himself thought to be mad. The other morning, after the Convair dived into the East River, an official of the Civil Aeronautics Board said that the plane was "on course and every circumstance was normal"—a true statement, aeronautically speaking. It was one of those statements, though, that illuminate the new normalcy, and it encouraged us to examine the affair more closely, to see how far the world has drifted toward accepting the miraculous as the commonplace. Put yourself, for a moment, at the Convair's controls and let us take a look at this day's normalcy. The speed of a Convair, approaching an airport, is about a hundred and

E.B. WHITE

forty miles an hour, or better than two miles a minute. We don't know the weight of the plane, but let us say that it is heavier than a grand piano. There are passengers aboard. The morning is dark, drizzly. The skies they are ashen and sober. You are in the overcast. Below, visibility is half a mile. (A few minutes ago it was a mile, but things have changed rather suddenly.) If your forward speed is two miles per minute and you can see half a mile after you get out of the overcast, that means you'll be able to see what you're in for in the next fifteen seconds. At the proper moment, you break out of the overcast and, if you have normal curiosity, you look around to see what's cooking. What you see, of course, is Queens—an awful shock at any time, and on this day of rain, smoke, and shifting winds a truly staggering shock. You are close to earth now, doing two miles a minute, every circumstance is normal, and you have a fifteen-second spread between what you *can* see and what you can't. What you hope to see, of course, is Runway 22 rising gently to kiss your wheels, but, as the passenger from Bath so

Notes on Our Times

aptly put it, "When I felt water splashing over my feet, I knew it wasn't an airport."

Airplane design has, it seems to us, been fairly static, and designers have docilely accepted the fixed-wing plane as the sensible and natural form. Improvements have been made in it, safety devices have been added, and strict rules govern its flight. But we'd like to see plane designers start playing with ideas less rigid than those that now absorb their fancy. The curse of flight is speed. Or, rather, the curse of flight is that no opportunity exists for dawdling. And so weather is still an enormous factor in air travel. Planes encountering fog are diverted to other airports, and set their passengers down hundreds of miles from where they want to be. In very bad weather, planes are not permitted to leave the ground at all. There are still plenty of people who refuse to fly simply because they don't like to proceed at two miles a minute through thick conditions. Before flight becomes what it ought to be, a new sort of plane will have to be created—perhaps a cross between a helicopter and a fixed-wing machine. Its virtue will be that its power can be used either to propel it rapidly forward or to sustain it vertically. So armed, this airplane will be able to face bad weather with equanimity, and when a pall of melancholy hangs over Queens, this plane will be seen creeping slowly down through the overcast and making a painstaking inspection of Runway 22, instead of coming in like a grand piano.

The above remarks on flying drew a fine letter from a T.W.A. captain. His observations reveal a man so well adjusted to this life that they deserve being published. It isn't every day that you encounter a serene personality, either on land or in the sky. The captain did not take exception to our rather sour view of heavier-than-air flight; he merely testified that the acceptance of aerial hazards made him feel "time-fitted" to his profession and "apt to our second of history." (Stylist as well as pilot.)

Notes on Our Times

> To move at a high rate of speed; to feel less secure the closer I come to earth and man; to be able to look ahead with some certainty for 15 seconds;—these factors characterize life in the world today. For most people this constitutes a constant hardship, including a rebellion and fretfulness against life. I suspect that by not merely accepting an unforeseeable future, but by building it into my life I may come closer to living a "normal" 20th century life than those who must still struggle against it.

Well, there you have birdman and philosopher rolled into one—the contemplative pilot, full of semicolons, perfectly sympathetic to modern urgencies, a man with a built-in unforeseeable future who has surrendered himself to his speedy century as proudly and passionately as a bride to her lover. He would be our choice of a pilot if we had to go anywhere by air. Happily, however, our own mind is quiet today, and we shall travel afoot in the Park, time-fitted to the life of a weekly hack, unfretful, grateful for the next fifteen seconds.

E.B. WHITE

The mental poise of this airline pilot in the middle of difficult flight shows man's spirit maintaining a small but significant lead over his instrument panel. Our own earthbound life, we realize, is schizophrenic. Half the time we feel blissfully wedded to the modern scene, in love with its every mood, amused by its every joke, imperturbable in the face of its threat, bent on enjoying it to the hilt. The other half of the time we are the fusspot moralist, suspicious of all progress, resentful of change, determined to right wrongs, correct injustices, and save the world even if we have to blow it to pieces in the process. These two characters war incessantly in us, and probably in most men. First one is on top, then the other—body and soul always ravaged by the internal slugging match. We envy Captain X, who has come out a whole man instead of a divided one and who is at peace with his environment. We envy all who fly with him through the great sky.

Railroads

There seems to be no reason to fear that any disturbing improvement in the railroads' condition will set in.

Notes on Our Times

The strong streak of insanity in railroads, which accounts for a child's instinctive feeling for them and for a man's unashamed devotion to them, is congenital; there seems to be no reason to fear that any disturbing improvement in the railroads' condition will set in. Lying at peace but awake in a Pullman berth all one hot night recently, we followed with dreamy satisfaction the familiar symphony of the cars—the diner departing (*furioso*) at midnight, the long, fever-laden silences between runs, the timeless gossip of rail and wheel during the runs, the crescendos and diminuendos, the piffling poop-pooping of the diesel's horn. For the most part, railroading is unchanged from our childhood. The water in which one washes one's face at morn is still without any real wetness, the little ladder leading to the upper is still the symbol of the tremendous adventure of the night, the green clothes hammock still sways with the curves, and there is still no foolproof place to store one's trousers.

E. B. WHITE

Our journey really began several days earlier, at the ticket window of a small station in the country, when the agent showed signs of cracking under the paperwork. "It's hard to believe," he said, "that after all these years I still got to write the word 'Providence' in here every time I make out one of these things. Now, there's no possible conceivable way you could make this journey *without* going through Providence, yet the Company wants the word written in here just the same. O.K., here she goes!" He gravely wrote "Providence" in the proper space, and we experienced anew the reassurance that rail travel is unchanged and unchanging, and that it suits our temperament perfectly—a dash of lunacy, a sense of detachment, not much speed, and no altitude whatsoever.

Mantis

We cannot guess what she prayed for, what she asked: possibly that a dressing table in a city apartment might prove to be a suitable place for depositing eggs.

Notes on Our Times

We found the corpse of a praying mantis on our wife's dressing table the other day and were more than commonly interested in the discovery, since we have been praying lately ourself, and if we were to die suddenly, our remains would probably look as comical in supplication, as dry and light. The mantis (a female) measured three and five-eighths inches from eye to tip of folded wings—a truly formidable bug. Her legs and the leading edge of her wings still held their beautiful grass-green color, and her thorax was the rich, ruddy-brown color of cornstalks. In fact, the mantis, in her desiccated condition, was curiously vegetable-like, a sort of animated twig (animated in retrospect, that is). Her arms were still in the attitude of prayer, her chin resting on one hand in perfect piety. We cannot guess what she prayed for, what she asked: possibly that a dressing table in a city apartment might prove to be a suitable place for depositing eggs. Our own prayers have been of great violence recently; we have implored God to strike down evil persons who are deliberately stirring

E.B. WHITE

up a rumpus and creating situations of incalculable mischief for the world. These are idle prayers, or at least badly conceived, and, like the mantis, we may die praying; but many people are muttering such prayers these days, and earnestly. In prayer, we feel more angry than religious.

Withholding

> There is, furthermore,
> a bad psychological effect
> in earning money that you
> never get your paws on.

Notes on Our Times

We have given about a year's thought to the withholding principle of taxation (not to be confused with the pay-as-you-go plan) and are now ready with our conclusion. Our belief is that withholding is a bad way to go about collecting tax money, even though the figures may show that it gets results. It is bad because it implies that the individual is incapable of handling his own affairs. The government as much as says: We know that, if left to your own devices, you will fritter away your worldly goods and tax day will catch you without cash. Or it says: We're not sure you'll come clean in your return, so we will just take the money before it reaches you and you will be saved the trouble and fuss of being honest. This implication is an unhealthy thing to spread around, being contrary to the old American theory that the individual is a very competent little guy indeed. The whole setup of our democratic government assumes that the citizen is bright, honest, and at least as fundamentally sound as a common stock. If you start treating him as something less than that, you are going to get into deep water, in our opinion. The device of withholding tax money, which is clearly confiscatory, since the individual is not allowed to see, taste, or touch a certain percentage of his wages, tacitly brands him as negligent or unthrifty or immature or incompetent or dishonest, or all of those things at once. There is, furthermore, a bad psychological effect in earning money that you never get your paws on. We believe this effect to be much stronger than the government realizes. At any rate, if the American individual is in truth incapable of paying his tax all by himself, then he should certainly be regarded as incapable of voting all by himself, and the Secretary of the Treasury should accompany him into the booth to show him where to put the X.

Nails

> We felt that if we should close quickly on them we'd get the sudden taste of lobster.

Notes on Our Times

Painted fingernails used to be the mark of the abandoned woman, but they have come a long way in a single generation and a lot of girls now paint their nails who haven't abandoned anything except a couple of bucks for the paint set. The other morning we visited our dental emporium to get our choppers cleaned, and as we reclined in the arms of the female oral hygienist, we were surprised to note that even *her* nails had been painted. Red as a rich man's barn, they insinuated themselves cleverly into our mouth and we felt that if we should close quickly on them we'd get the sudden taste of lobster. And not long ago we had some blood removed from our arm in a hospital and the nurse who tapped us had blood-red nails, as though she had dipped them daintily in our lifestream, as in a fingerbowl. Since there is nothing prettier than a pretty hand, we often wonder why women persist in messing themselves up that way—the same sort of impulse, no doubt, that causes some people to desecrate the lovely shell of a young turtle by painting the Statue of Liberty on it.

Crab Grass

> Mr. Brinckerhoff has taken the pressure off crab grass and off himself: he has come up with the discovery that you can just leave the stuff alone and survive; you don't have to fight it.

Notes on Our Times

With lawnmowing just about over for the year, it was a pleasure the other morning to find a letter in the *Tribune* in defense of crab grass. The letter was from Mr. Gilbert G. Brinckerhoff, a retired schoolteacher living in Radburn, New Jersey, and it was the first piece of original thinking we had come across in weeks. Mr. Brinckerhoff, probably alone among homeowners in the United States, has taken the pressure off crab grass and off himself: he has come up with the discovery that you can just leave the stuff alone and survive; you don't have to fight it. Brinckerhoff has developed a lawn that is one hundred per cent crab grass; not a spear of anything else mars its lovely green surface. It makes, he says, a very presentable lawn. What this discovery will do to the Scott Lawn Company, what steps against Brinckerhoff will be taken by an aroused citizenry of Radburn—these are subjects for conjecture. But at least there is one man in America whose energies are not flowing into silly channels and who can stand erect and look something in the face. We admire Brinckerhoff and wish him a long, indolent retirement, much of which can be spent in a rocker on the porch overlooking the weedy plain.

Remembrance of Things Past

Farmers who have experimented
with the artificial method
of raising pigs have discovered
that it is advisable to retain one
link with nature—one
remembrance of things past.

Notes on Our Times

These are the antibiotic days, when even newborn pigs are removed to sanitary surroundings, to be raised on laboratory milk, innocent of any connection with the sow. Pigs are "hatched" nowadays, rather than farrowed. After a few brief swigs of colostrum, they are transferred to the brooder, where an electric heat lamp comforts them, and where they are soon nuzzling the great, many-teated breasts of science and drinking an elixir of terramycin, skim milk, and concentrated vim. (How much of the terramycin finds its way to the consumer in ham and pork, to plague those who have an allergy to that drug and to lower everyone's resistance to Virus X, has not been demonstrated.)

Farmers who have experimented with the artificial method of raising pigs have discovered that it is advisable to retain one link with nature—one remembrance of things past. So the modern pig nursery is equipped with a record-player, and at proper intervals the infants hear the victrola give forth the sounds of suckling—the blissful grunting of sows as they let down their milk. The little pigs respond. A chord is touched. They awake and feed.

Man's separation from his mother, Nature, is quite parallel to the pig's from the sow. The separation, it seems, becomes more complete with every passing year, and may finally reach the point of artifice where, to maintain life at all, we will have to resort to a recording—some recollection of the natural world, some grunting noise that takes us back to reality and stirs us to accept the half-forgotten sources of our original supply.

Experimentation

The desire to toss something in a new way, or to toss it a greater distance, is fairly steady in men and boys.

Notes on Our Times

The year ends on a note of pure experimentation. Dr. Fritz Zwicky last week tried to hurl some metal slugs out into space, free of the earth's gravitational pull. Dr. Zwicky stood in New Mexico and tossed from there. He was well equipped: he had a rocket that took the slugs for the first forty-mile leg of the journey and then discharged them at high velocity to continue on their own. The desire to toss something in a new way, or to toss it a greater distance, is fairly steady in men and boys. Boys stand on high bridges, chucking chips down wind, or they stand on the shore of a pond, tossing rocks endlessly at a floating bottle, or at a dead cat, observing closely every detail of their experiment, trying to make every stone sail free of the pull of past experience. Then the boys grow older, stand in the desert, still chucking, observing, wondering. They have almost exhausted the earth's possibilities and are going on into the empyrean to throw at the stars, leaving the earth's people frightened and joyless, and leaving some fellow scientists switching over from science to politics and hoping they have made the switch in time.

Daylight and Darkness

The consequences of the
atomic cataclysm that are being
relentlessly published seem
mild alongside the wry smell of
chrysanthemums in the air.

Notes on Our Times

Up early this day, trying to decide whether or not to bequeath our brain to our alma mater, which is making a collection of such stuff. It struck us as odd that the decision will have to be made by the brain itself and that no other part of us—a foot or a gall bladder—can be in on the matter, although all are, in a way, concerned. Our head is small and we fear that our brain may suffer by comparison if arranged on a shelf with others. Spent part of the morning composing an inscription to go with our brain, but all we got was this:

> Observe, quick friend, this quiet noodle,
> This kit removed from its caboodle.
> Here sits a brain at last unhinged,
> On which too many thoughts impinged.

Spent the rest of the morning studying the crisis in the newspapers and watching apple-fall and leaf-fall in our city backyard, where nature is cleverly boxed and has therefore an appearance of special value, as of a jewel so precious that it must always be suitably contained. The day was clear, with a gentle wind, and the small leaves descended singly and serenely, except now and then when a breeze entered and caused a momentary rain of leaves—what one weather prophet on the radio calls "inner mitten" showers. A school of fish paraded slowly counterclockwise in the fountain, and on the wall above us hung seed pods of the polygonum vine. Our complaint about the crisis is not that it is so appalling but that it is so trivial. The consequences of the atomic cataclysm that are being relentlessly published seem mild alongside the burning loveliness of a fall morning, or the flash of a southbound bird, or the wry smell of chrysanthemums in the air. We examined everything said yesterday in the council chambers of the mighty and could find not a single idea that was not trifling, not a noble word of any calibre, not one unhurried observation or natural thought. The newspaper headline prophesying darkness is less moving than the pool of daylight that overflows upon it from the window, illuminating it. The light of day—so hard at times to see, so convincing when seen.

Air Raid Drill

It occurred to us, gliding by
the thirteenth floor and seeing
the numeral "14" painted on it,
that our atom-splitting scientists
had committed the error of
impatience and had run on ahead
of the rest of the human race.

Notes on Our Times

Five minutes after the all-clear sounded, everyone on our floor of *The New Yorker* offices was back at work. Nobody escaped, in the confusion, to another part of the city or to another planet; nobody tried to prolong the recess period in order to savor his freedom; none seemed desirous of meditating on the heavy implications of an A-bomb drill. To slip back into harness—that was the compelling aim. It was the same story all through the city—eight million well-behaved citizens, docile as lambs, huddled in hallways and tunnels while a hush fell over all. The city fathers were delighted, as indeed they might be. Yet how discouraging, really, such behavior is! It might have been more promising for the future had we all rushed wildly into the streets, punched wardens in the nose, and screamed our defiance of the implausible and crazy design that had led us to this pretty pass. But there was no sign of that. Only one fellow, of all we heard about, questioned the normality of eight million people creeping into the walls like mice. He stepped out on Broadway, gazed up and down, and asked, "What's this—something new?"

We inmates of the nineteenth floor were supposed to proceed, by easy stages, to the tenth floor, and that is exactly what we did. Bubbling with good spirits and bright as birds, we assembled at the elevators and were piped aboard, in lots of a dozen, for the weird descent to the survival chamber, or tenth-floor corridor. This descent from the nineteenth to the tenth is, in our building, the dodge that has been agreed upon as the means of eluding the atom—a queer piece of magic but one that is probably as good as any other. The tenth floor is an important station on the lift, being the first express stop, and in a few minutes the corridor of the tenth was full of people. Cars discharged passengers briskly. There was an overtone of uneasy mirth, rising to a slightly exaggerated pitch, as though each of us had had one cocktail. There was a temptation to clown, reminiscent of grammar-school days, when a fire drill brought sudden relief from classroom tedium. Underneath the

Notes on Our Times

mirth and chatter, easily discernible in the faces, was the deep current of loneliness, of fear—the imagination, carefully controlled at the surface level, operating miles down in the dark unfathomable regions.

Our descent from the nineteenth floor to the tenth floor was, we realized, a drop not of nine flights but of eight. This building has no floor called "13"; hence the "fourteenth" floor is a euphemism, and all the other floors above the twelfth are numbered not by a system of mathematics but by witchcraft. In our descent, then, in the cheerful lift, we not only had to evade an atomic explosion by taking a short journey but we had to subtract ten from nineteen and get eight. It occurred to us, gliding by the thirteenth floor and seeing the numeral "14" painted on it, that our atom-splitting scientists had committed the error of impatience and had run on ahead of the rest of the human race. They had dared look into the core of the sun, and had fiddled with it; but it might have been a good idea if they had waited to do that until the rest of us could look the number 13 square in the face. Such is the true nature of our peculiar dilemma.

For a minute or two during our sojourn on the tenth floor, we tried to take stock of our life, tried to understand what had brought us to this ignominious pass. We wondered whether the very qualities that are so generally admired—industry, ingenuity, loyalty, faith—whether they had not played a big part in it. Centuries of good behavior, centuries of brilliant achievement in the arts and sciences, and we take cover in a steel-and-plaster corridor, standing erect and tractable in fantastic assemblage, next to those we love, to await the messy results of some basic mismanagement, some distant fury, some essential cruelty and bestiality.

The papers reported that millions of dollars in manpower were lost by the quiescence of eight million persons. For fifteen minutes, wealth ran down the drain. This, like the missing thirteenth floor, was a mathematical enigma that stopped us

Notes on Our Times

cold. What happened, exactly? Who lost what? How can anyone say for sure that millions of dollars were lost? Probably the dollars, like the people, were not lost—just deeply troubled. Like the people, the dollars stood still for a brief while. For a quarter of an hour, no citizen, no dollar, did anything much. Travel, busy-ness, creation, connivance, promotion, shopping—all were at low ebb. It was eerie, but it was not necessarily a loss. The Consolidated Edison Company noted a sharp dip in the curve of kilowattage, giving stockholders a nasty turn but relieving consumers of fifteen minutes of expensive electrical existence. It was one of those intense moments (as at midnight on December 31st) when it is hard to say what, precisely, is taking place. People are so addicted to activity that the sudden stoppage of it gives them a quick sense of something being wrong, when, in point of fact, it may be the beginning of something being right.

A fellow we stood next to in the corridor, and who survived, confided to us that the drill was costing *The New Yorker* a pretty penny, because at that very moment a couple of high-priced lawyers were in the office and they were being paid by the hour. But what he failed to say was whether the advice they were peddling was good or bad. If it should turn out to be bad, then every minute they were rendered inarticulate was so much gain. We regard the published estimates of community loss during the test as highly suspect. Who knows? Maybe if everybody in the world stood still for a quarter of an hour and looked into the eyes of the next man, the mischief would come to an end.

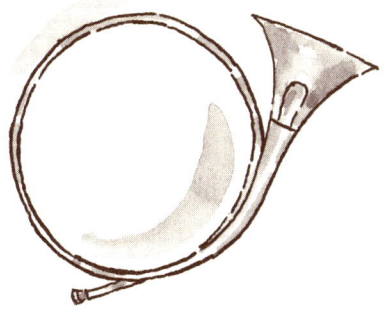

The Distant Music of the Hounds

> The miracle of Christmas is
> that, like the distant and very
> musical voice of the hound,
> it penetrates finally and
> becomes heard in the heart.

Notes on Our Times

To perceive Christmas through its wrapping becomes more difficult with every year. There was a little device we noticed in one of the sporting-goods stores—a trumpet that hunters hold to their ears so that they can hear the distant music of the hounds. Something of the sort is needed now to hear the incredibly distant sound of Christmas in these times, through the dark, material woods that surround it. "Silent Night," canned and distributed in thundering repetition in the department stores, has become one of the greatest of all noisemakers, almost like the rattles and whistles of Election Night. We rode down on an escalator the other morning through the silent-nighting of the loudspeakers, and the man just in front of us was singing, "I'm gonna wash this store right outa my hair, I'm gonna wash this store…"

The miracle of Christmas is that, like the distant and very musical voice of the hound, it penetrates finally and becomes heard in the heart—over so many years, through so many cheap curtain-raisers. It is not destroyed even by all the arts and craftiness of the destroyers, having an essential simplicity that is everlasting and triumphant, at the end of confusion. We once went out at night with coon-hunters and we were aware that it was not so much the promise of the kill that took the men away from their warm homes and sent them through the cold shadowy woods, it was something more human, more mystical—something even simpler. It was the night, and the excitement of the note of the hound, first heard, then not heard. It was the natural world, seen at its best and most haunting, unlit except by stars, impenetrable except to the knowing and the sympathetic.

Christmas in this year of crisis must compete as never before with the dazzling complexity of man, whose tangential desires and ingenuities have created a world that gives any simple thing the look of obsolescence—as though there were something inherently foolish in what is simple, or natural. The human brain is about to turn certain functions over to an efficient substitute, and we hear of a robot that is now capable

Notes on Our Times

of handling the tedious details of psychoanalysis, so that the patient no longer need confide in a living doctor but can take his problems to a machine, which sifts everything and whose "brain" has selective power and the power of imagination. One thing leads to another. The machine that is imaginative will, we don't doubt, be heir to the ills of the imagination; one can already predict that the machine itself may become sick emotionally, from strain and tension, and be compelled at last to consult a medical man, whether of flesh or of steel. We have tended to assume that the machine and the human brain are in conflict. Now the fear is that they are indistinguishable. Man not only is notably busy himself but insists that the other animals follow his example. A new bee has been bred artificially, busier than the old bee.

So this day and this century proceed toward the absolutes of convenience, of complexity, and of speed, only occasionally holding up the little trumpet (as at Christmas time) to be reminded of the simplicities, and to hear the distant music of

E. B. WHITE

the hound. Man's inventions, directed always onward and upward, have an odd way of leading back to man himself, as a rabbit track in snow leads eventually to the rabbit. It is one of his more endearing qualities that man should think his tracks lead outward, toward something else, instead of back around the hill to where he has already been; and it is one of his persistent ambitions to leave earth entirely and travel by rocket into space, beyond the pull of gravity, and perhaps try another planet, as a pleasant change. He knows that the atomic age is capable of delivering a new package of energy; what he doesn't know is whether it will prove to be a blessing. This week, many will be reminded that no explosion of atoms generates so hopeful a light as the reflection of a star, seen appreciatively in a pasture pond. It is there we perceive Christmas—and the sheep quiet, and the world waiting.

The Photographs

The Underwood typewriter that appears in the photograph on the endpapers of this book belonged to E. B. White. The typewriter is housed at Cornell University, and the photograph is reproduced by kind permission of the Division of Rare and Manuscript Collections, Cornell University Library. This photograph also served as the basis for the illustration on the cover of the book.

The photograph of E. B. White shows the author in his office at *The New Yorker* with his dachshund Minnie. It is reproduced by permission of The New York Times/Redux.

Uncommon Books for Serious Readers

Boston
Henry Cabot Lodge

A Boy at the Hogarth Press
Written and illustrated by
Richard Kennedy

Delight
J. B. Priestley

The Dream
Sir Winston Churchill

Feeding the Mind
Lewis Carroll

A Fortnight in the Wilderness
Alexis de Tocqueville

**Jerusalem: The Saga of
the Holy City**
Benjamin Mazar et al.

**The Little Guide to Your
Well-Read Life**
Steve Leveen

The Making of The Finest Hour
Speech by Winston S. Churchill
Introduction by
Richard M. Langworth

New York
Theodore Roosevelt

On a Life Well Spent
Cicero
Preface by Benjamin Franklin

Painting as a Pastime
Winston S. Churchill

Samuel Johnson's Dictionary
Selections from the 1755 work
that defined the English language
Edited by Jack Lynch

Samuel Johnson's Insults
Edited by Jack Lynch

The Silverado Squatters
Six selected chapters
Robert Louis Stevenson

**Sir Winston Churchill's Life
Through His Paintings**
David Coombs
with Minnie Churchill
Foreword by Mary Soames

Levenger Press is the publishing arm of

Levenger.com   800.544.0880